Bible Trek

Reading the Bible in Thirteen Weeks

Juel A. Fitzgerald

Juel's Creations, LLC

Copyright © 2021

All rights reserved. No part of this publication may be reproduced, distributed or transmitted in any form or by any means, without prior written permission.

Scripture taken from the Holy Bible, New International Version®, NIV® Copyright ©1973, 1978, 1984, 2011 by Biblica, Inc.® Used by permission. All rights reserved worldwide.

Quote taken from "The Bible in 90 Days Cover-to-Cover in 12 Pages a Day" Copyright © 1996, 2005. Used by permission of Zondervan. www.zondervan.com.

Juel's Creations, LLC
P. O. Box 221172
Beachwood, OH 44122
https://juelscreations.com

Book Layout © 2016 BookDesignTemplates.com
Book Cover © 2021 designed by Andre A. Morgan, III.

Book Title/ Author Name. -- 1st ed.
ISBN: 978-1-7348583-3-4

Acknowledgements

It was not my plan to create this book of devotionals. My plan was to create a much larger book of devotionals. However, because of God's nudging two smaller books in addition to other books of devotionals will exist. Thank you, Lord, for Your direction, Your plan, and Your purpose.

Thanks to both my parents, James and Kathryn Taylor, who led me in the way I should go.

Thanks to my editor, Derek Dixon. He catches what I miss after I edit.

Thanks to Andre A. Morgan, Graphic Designer, for the creation of the book cover.

Lastly thanks to Bobbi Brown who God used to encourage me to take this Bible Trek journey.

Contents

Introduction	i
Week One – Family Drama Excursions	1
Week Two – Escape to Godly Order?	7
Week Three – Which Highway?	11
Week Four – The Carried Relationships	15
Week Five – Journey of a Great King	19
Week Six – The Rocky Road	23
Week Seven – The Road to Peace	29
Week Eight – What Time Is It?	33
Week Nine – Distractions Along the Way	37
Week Ten – Messengers Trekking Along	41
Week Eleven – I Am with You	47
Week Twelve – The Public Figure	51
Week Thirteen – The Scattered Letters	55

Introduction

I have always wanted to read the Bible from cover to cover. However, I could never finish reading the Bible using any of the one-year plans. Twelve months is a long time. Some time during that year, I would get distracted by life issues, get bored, or fall asleep. It seems the year dragged with no light at the end of the tunnel.

Then Bobbi, a sister from my church, challenged a small group us to join her on reading the Bible in 90 days. I thought she was crazy.

"How am I going to make 90 days when I can't make it through a whole year?" I whined.

"It's quicker, no deep study, just absorbing the facts as you follow the 90-Day plan." She said to convince me to take this adventure with her.

We used "The Bible in 90 Days Cover-to-Cover in 12 Pages a Day" a Zondervan creation using the New International Version. This Bible is broken up into eighty-eight days with twelve pages each day. Two days are left open at the end in case there is a need to miss two days during this three-month journey; these are called "grace days". Therefore, if no days are missed the completion of the Bible could be done in eighty-eight days. Zondervan's goal is "to read attentively every word of the Bible in 90 days."

At the start of this time, we were to prepare ourselves by scanning over the Bible to see how it was structured and review the reading plan. Then at the start of each day's reading, Zondervan suggested we say the following brief prayer: "Gracious Father, thank You for the gift that I hold in my hands. May Your Spirit fill me and interpret Your precious words for me as I read them. In Your Son's name I pray, Amen." I do not recall saying this specific prayer every day, but I am sure I prayed before starting this crazy adventure.

Bobbi and I chose a three-month period in the Summer of 2007 when our schedule was least full. It would have been harder for me to take on this trek filled with meetings, work, schooling etc. At that time, I was a full-time government employee, part time student at Kent State University, mother, wife, grandparent, and part-time travel agent. I also had my toes in two other network marketing endeavors.

During this trip, we were not to do any deep analyses, studies, cross referencing, concordance use or any other Bible tools we normally would have while reading the Bible. The purpose was to merely read God's Word at the rate of twelve pages per day. However, if some question or thought did pop into our brains, we were to write a note for further reference at another time. Twelve pages per day is a long distance, and no distractions were allowed to veer us off course. Our focus was to be that of former detective drama "Dragnet" Joe Friday's "just the facts, ma'am".

The trek was different than any other reading. Blazing through the bible at this faster-but-more-manageable rate helped show me the flow of the Bible and what was in it. I jotted down any unanticipated revelations (no pun intended). I do not recall Bobbi and I having a discussion while we read. I think we let each other know where we were. My goal was to finish in the eighty-eight days, which we both did. Somehow, we did not need the grace days. Even if I fell behind, somehow, I caught back up. Also, I did something different: Since this was my first time doing this, I decided to do it with an amplified audio Bible so I could hear, feel, and see the scriptures. The amplified Bible had all the sound effects of the time period in the text. Plus, it gave me the opportunity to learn the correct pronunciations of the names and places. While I listened, I read along. To hear from God's Word the sounds of horses and other animals, whips, people screaming, and whatever else was pure joy. I felt like I was there at every scene. It made the Word come to life.

I loved this adventure so much that I did it three more years during the Summer. The second year, I took on the challenge of using the "The Bible in 90 Days Cover-to-Cover in 12 Pages a Day" with my own eyes and not listening to audio. The third year, I used the "New Revised Standard" version; and in the fourth year, I used the "Today's New International" version. Bobbi also took on the challenge annually. She even tried to use the "King James" version. I did not try that version because I knew I would get lost in the language. I was raised reading that version, but it can be brain-numbing.

Something happened in my life that stopped the annual Summer reads through the Bible: The fourth year, 2010, was the year before I retired. I realize that when God takes me on a journey, it indicates the present time is done and He is preparing me to move to another place for His purpose. Writing this book now almost makes me want to do a fifth trip, which might be from nostalgia. However, if it is a prompting by the Holy Spirit, it will happen. The perfect 90-day period will materialize.

By using "The Bible in 90 Days Cover-to-Cover in 12 Pages a Day", anyone can read the bible within 90 days. It is an adventure that will thrill, inform, shock, reveal, sicken, and marvel the reader. It is a journey everyone should take at least once.

In 2010, God used a trip to California for a writer's conference to compel me to plunge into the world of spiritual devotional blogging. My first few entries were about that fourth year 90-day journey in the Bible. For thirteen weeks, I wrote briefly about that week's reading. I encourage you to use the "The Bible in 90 Days Cover-to-Cover in 12 Pages a Day" and then read each week's devotional in this book. Keep in mind the readings here will not be deep nor include cross references, just the facts of what was read that week. May this be the beginning of your own annual 90-day trek through the Bible.

Family Drama Excursions

What was I thinking? Unlike the prior three years when I took this same journey through the Bible, I got off to a slow start. Maybe it was because of my recent return from Los Angeles. Maybe it was because I worked extra hours. Maybe it is because of wanting to record this journey for others to read. It started slow, but I am on schedule to catch up.

The journey began in Genesis where it was fascinating to watch how God created everything in the world simply by speaking it into existence (except for mankind, whom He fashioned with His hands) "God saw all that he had made, and it was very good." (Genesis 1:31a).

I mourned with Eve because she would never know what it means to have a painless childbirth and she and Adam were thrown out of paradise. On top of that, their two sons were at odds with each other to the point that Cain killed his brother, Abel. The first murder in the Bible. (Genesis 3-4).

The world must have been incredibly awful for God to be so aggrieved:

> ... how great the wickedness of the human race had become on the earth, and that every inclination of the thoughts of the human heart was only evil all the time. (Genesis 6:5).

He had such regret about creating humans that He planned to wipe them from the earth. He flooded the earth and, through His servant, Noah, saved only those animals and humans in the ark and creatures in the sea whom God mandated. (Genesis 6-9)

I was reminded of how, even at a mature age, we can be as useful to God as Abraham and Sarah were. I was baptized into God's church when I was forty-one. At that time, I wished I could have truly known God when I was younger and maybe I would not have suffered the grief of my sins. I was a member of many churches since childhood, but I did not walk with Him. I did what I wanted. However, I have come to learn that God's timing is perfect, and He calls us at specific times for His divine purpose. All we need to do is answer His call.

Both Abraham and Sarah were old when He told them to leave for a foreign land. Both were old when they had Isaac;

Abraham was one hundred and Sarah was ninety or ninety-one. This was part of God's promise to Abraham to...

> . . . make you into a great nation, and I will bless you; I will make your name great, and you will be a blessing. I will bless those who bless you and whoever curses you I will curse; and all peoples on earth will be blessed through you. (Genesis 12:2-3).

Abraham's faith was deep, and it was credited to him as righteousness. I would love to say I have that same type of faith, but I do not think I would be willing to sacrifice my son like Abraham was. Despite Abraham's faith, he was a sinner like us all. He and Sarah lied twice because of fear and said Sarah was his sister. They used a servant to produce Ishmael because they could not wait for God's promise to be fulfilled. This lack of patience led to strife between the two women and Abraham for the rest of their lives. We are the same when we take our eyes off God's plans and go our own way. We allow fear and lack of patience to misdirect us. That affects us and others. (Genesis 12-18, 20-23)

When God had to destroy the evil in Sodom and Gomorrah, I was surprised at how Lot hesitated about leaving Sodom. He had to be dragged out with his family. Somehow, I missed that in my prior readings. I was so focused on his wife and how she looked back and turned to a pillar of salt.

Are we ready to go when God tells us to, even if it means leaving everything? (Genesis 19)

God never followed the norms of man by giving the first born the birthright for several individuals in Genesis. One of them was Jacob. Isaac's wife was pregnant and there was so much movement in her womb that she asked God what was happening.

> The Lord said to her, "Two nations are in your womb, and two peoples from within you will be separated; one people will be stronger than the other and older will serve the younger." (Genesis 25:23).

Even though Isaac wanted Esau to have the birthright and the blessing, God used the sins of Isaac, Rebekah, Esau, and Jacob to fulfill His promise of Esau serving Jacob. Isaac loved Esau more and Rebekah loved Jacob more. This favoritism created jealousy, hatred, and ill will in the family. I wonder what would have happened if Isaac and Rebekah had talked with God first to find out what His plan was instead of taking matters into their own hands, not favoring one son over another. (Genesis 24, 27-28)

The creation of the twelve tribes of Israel was made through Jacob, Leah, Rachel, and two servants. Jacob had two wives because Laban tricked him into marrying Leah, the older daughter, when Jacob was in love with Rachel, the younger daughter. Whatever love existed between the sisters after they were married to Jacob disappeared due to jealousy and the desire to be loved. It perplexes me how we allow the intense love of one child over another to affect the family. In Jacob's case, God used this for their good through one of his younger sons, Joseph. God used challenges in Joseph's life to enable him to save the lives of the family during an intense famine. (Genesis 37, 39-47)

Fear of a nation, not of their kind, was displayed by the Egyptians by their enslavement of the Israelites. Despite intense oppression, the Israelites continued to multiply. The king of Egypt then told the Hebrew midwives to kill any boys born. However, because of their fear of God, they told the king that Hebrew women are tough, and the babies were born before they arrived. Birth, survival, a murderous act, and hearing God in a burning bush about His plan to free the Israelites were all revealed to Moses. (Exodus 1-3)

Trekking through Genesis and the first three chapters of Exodus show that life dramas existed and still exist today in our families. This is a reminder to be reliant on the strength of God alone and not the frailty of ourselves.

WEEK TWO – EXODUS 4 TO NUMBERS 25

Escape to Godly Order?

Moses was a reluctant leader. I can relate. It is not often I volunteer for a service in my community without being asked. Somehow God convinces me that He needs me for His purpose at whatever venue He chooses. Through Moses, God freed His people from Egypt. We see His power through ten plagues of blood, frogs, gnats, flies, death of livestock, boils, hail, locust, darkness, and death of all who were firstborn. Our mouths dropped when we saw the Lord divide the sea so that the Israelites could cross on dry land; and watched as Pharaoh's army perished when they tried to do the same. The Ten Commandments and other laws from God came into existence. (Exodus 4-14, 20-31)

God was firm on total obedience. Sin was met with negative consequences; however, He was forgiving. It amazes me that Aaron, the one who encouraged the golden calf to be built in Exodus, was His first priest. Maybe God had to use him as the example for atoning for his own sins and the sins of others for the rest of his life. (Exodus 32)

After losing fifty-three pounds, I came to the realization that God instructed the Israelites in

Leviticus to use olive oil in making offerings holy. A small amount of olive oil is one of the healthy oils a person needs daily in their life. It is interesting that God chose that oil for their pleasing and aromatic offerings.

The list of clean and unclean foods in Leviticus 11 continues to give me pause on my current day application of what foods are permissible. Without a doubt, there are foods that are healthier for the physical body to consume than others. The part that always gets me is what God says in Lev. 11:9-10:

> Of all the creatures living in the water of the seas and the streams you may eat any that have fins and scales. But all creatures in the seas or streams that do not have fins and scales—whether among all the swarming things or among all the other living creatures in the water—you are to regard as unclean.

I love fish. I also love shrimp. Every time I see this, I wonder, should shrimp be taken out of my healthy living diet as I walk this life for God? When I think about the fact that shrimps are generally bottom dwellers, taking in toxins and other contaminants from the sea, it causes me to think twice about consuming them. Here, God says no. Granted, this was written in a different time; but has man justified disobeying God's command simply because shrimp tastes good? Shellfish allergies abound in our world today.

From Leviticus 12 until Leviticus 27, God provides standards for godly and clean living for His people. He knew through enslavement much had been lost and He wanted them to begin a righteous lifestyle with Him.

In Numbers 14:2-3, the Israelites whined after getting the report that the land flowed with milk and honey. Though the land was marvelous, overtaking it would be a great challenge due to the anticipated resistance from the inhabitants that possessed it:

> All the Israelites grumbled against Moses and Aaron, and the whole assembly said to them, "If only we had died in Egypt! Or in this wilderness! Why is the LORD bringing us to this land only to let us fall by the sword? Our wives and children will be taken as plunder. Wouldn't it be better for us to go back to Egypt?"

When God tells me to move into something more challenging (something out of my comfort zone), I so often cry, "Oh not *that*! Can't I just stay as I am? This which You ask is going to be so hard. I will look like an idiot if I fail!" Duh! If God is sending me, how can I fail? I am so thankful that He has never failed me when I have chosen to obey Him instead of staying in the desert of regret.

WEEK THREE – NUMBERS 25 TO I SAMUEL 2

Which Highway?

This week's trek through the Bible was spent up in the Shenandoah Mountains and down by the Chesapeake Bay. Living among God's nature in the forest, which was by the sea, we saw how nature is totally reliant on God for daily food and shelter as it perpetuates the life cycle governed by God. Being out of my sometimes-patterned lifestyle makes me reflect on whether I am living that governed life cycle God has laid out for me.

Am I being what He needs me to be?

- Am I worshiping Him and giving Him my daily, monthly, and annual offerings of my life, soul, finances -- everything I am simply because of His love for me and my love for him? (Numbers 28 to 29)
- Am I keeping my vows? (Numbers 30)
- Am I mindful of where God has taken me in my family and personal history, learned from it, and used it for my present and future only for God? (Number 33 – Deuteronomy 4)
- Am I being obedient to God's laws? (Deuteronomy 4 – 26)

- Am I totally reliant on God as nature is and allowing him to fight my battles for me? (Joshua 3 – 6, 8, 10 – 12)

Or do I forget my history and God's love (as the children of Israel did in Judges) and am swayed by the temptations of the world? Prayerfully, I am like Ruth, following God wherever He takes me and doing whatever He needs me to do. Hopefully, I am giving my children over to God like Hannah did.

When I think of Moses, I think of how God "buried him in Moab, in the valley opposite Beth Peor... no prophet has risen in Israel like Moses, whom the LORD knew face to face," (Deuteronomy. 34: 6,10). What makes my mouth drop about Moses is how God used him despite his weaknesses. Though he was not able to go into the Promised Land because of his slip of faith, God let him see the land from atop a mountain. What blows me away even more is that God personally buried him. No man laid Moses to rest, God did.

Being like Moses is huge as he sermonized in Deuteronomy:

Love the LORD your God with all your heart and with all your soul and with all your strength. These commandments that I give you today are to be on your hearts. Impress them on your children. Talk about them when you sit at home and when you walk along the road, when you lie down and when you get up. Tie them as symbols on your hands and bind them on your foreheads. Write them on the door frames of your houses and on your gates. (Deuteronomy 6:5-9).

It should be clear to all that I walk with God and He lives through me even when I am weak.

He is the God who hears and answers prayer. The barren Hannah never gave up in her prayers to the Lord. She prayed for a son and promised that she would give him to the Lord. God heard and answered her prayer with the birth of Samuel. When he was old enough to be weaned, she gave him to the Lord under the tutelage of Eli the priest. She bowed down in a prayer of praise to God for his blessings. I cannot imagine wanting a child so much that I would be willing to give him up for the Lord to use. This type of faith and deep relationship with God is always convicting. (I Samuel 1 and 2)

As a parent, I Samuel 2 reminds us how we are responsible for how our children are raised. Eli, the priest had two sons who defiled God's name with their bodies, showing no regard for

Him. However, Eli raised Samuel, another woman's son, in the ways of the Lord. The consequences for Eli's two sons were death on the same day. Eli had turned a blind eye to his children's behavior, and they suffered, Eli's strength was diminished and no one in his family line would reach old age. How proactive are we in directing our children in the ways of the Lord?

Which highway are we walking on, the one using God's GPS through His Word or our way?

WEEK FOUR — I SAMUEL 3 TO 2 SAMUEL 24

The Carried Relationships

This week's trek began after unpacking from a week in the mountains and a ride to the hospital emergency room in an ambulance from my job. A severe headache on the right side, strange vision on the left, accompanied with a slight tingling in the left limbs, and nausea preceded that unexpected medical adventure. While in a drugged stupor, I received the results — migraine and sinusitis. Thank goodness it was not what it originally appeared as -- a stroke. Therefore, I fell three days behind on the Bible trail. I was not concerned, though, because there would be time to catch up later.

I revisited David — one of God's anointed. When I think of David, I do not think of Goliath or about the songs about his many victories, "Saul has slain his thousands, and David his tens of thousands." (I Samuel 18:7). When I think of David, I think of relationships and family drama! It is a wonder how God told Samuel to "Rise and anoint him; this is the one." (I Samuel 16:12).

Though David was chosen by God, he is so like all of us — he struggled with his relationships.

As a boy, his oldest brother, Eliab, berated him by saying:

> Why have you come down here?... I know how conceited you are and how wicked your heart is; you came down only to watch the battle. (I Samuel 17:28).

Years later, after David took out Goliath with a stone and sling, Saul, Israel's first king, feared him and desired him dead, thus sending him into hiding. God worked this out, however, and made David king. His wife, Michal (Saul's daughter) "was in love with David" but later "despised him in her heart" (I Samuel 18:20 and 2 Samuel 6:16).

While staying home from one of his many battles as king, David slept with Bathsheba, another man's wife, and got her pregnant. When David could not convince the husband to sleep with his wife, to cover up the transgression, David put him on the front line to be killed, then married the woman. (2 Samuel 11-12) Is that deep or what? When I first read this a year ago, I could not believe this was the same David who slew Goliath. *That* same guy? no way!

Later Tamar, the sister of his son, Absalom, was raped by his other son

Amnon. I wonder what went through David's mind when he realized he had fallen into Amnon's scheme by telling Tamar to "Go to the house of your brother, Amnon, and prepare some food for him." (2 Sam 13:7). Then Absalom waited and killed his brother two years later for this violation. After some time, this same son of David plotted to take over his reign.

Yet, he had deep relationships with his mighty men and Jonathan. He was not shielded from having bizarre encounters with others simply because he was the "anointed one". So too, none of us are shielded from life's interactions with others simply because we are Christians. God used David like He uses all of us, despite the difficult or downright sinful interpersonal relationships with which we allow ourselves to become involved.

Through these trials, we grow, we learn, we mourn, we scream, and we repent, all to be pleasing in God's sight.

> The Lord is my rock, my fortress and my deliverer; my God is my rock in whom I take refuge, my shield and the horn of my salvation. He is my stronghold, my refuge and my savior—from violent people you save me. I called to the Lord, who is worthy of praise, and have been saved from my enemies. (2 Samuel 22:2-4)

How is our relationship with the Lord positively affecting our physical encounters with family, friends, and strangers? How does God's glory shine so much through us that others cannot help but see Him? How important is it that we please God and not others or ourselves?

WEEK FIVE – I KINGS TO 2 CHRONICLES 36:23

Journey of a Great King

Good morning, God. Thank You for this week's roaming through the last few chapters of the historical part of your Word. Thank You for the examples You provided me of spiritual leadership. Thank You for allowing me to see what is pleasing in Your sight.

King David is now old and feeble. One of his sons, Adonijah, thought it was a good time to take his place as King. He obtained support from all his brothers, except one, Solomon, and other community leaders and set himself up as king. When this was discovered, David was informed. He had Zadok the priest and Nathan the prophet to anoint his son Solomon as king according to God's will. This sent Adonijah and his cronies packing in fear.

David gave this charge to Solomon:

> "I am about to go the way of all the earth," he said. "So be strong, act like a man, and observe what the LORD your God requires: Walk in obedience to him, and keep his decrees and commands, his laws and regulations, as written in the Law of Moses. Do this so that you may prosper in all you do and wherever you go and that the LORD may keep his promise to me: 'If your descendants watch how they live, and if they walk faithfully before me with all their heart and soul, you will never fail to have a successor on the throne of Israel.'" I Kings 2:2-4.

With this charge, other instructions, and God being with him, Solomon became a great king. He asked God for wisdom. Because he only asked for wisdom, God gave him wisdom, wealth, and honor, superior to other kings, and promised if he would remain in obedience to God, he would have long life. King Solomon went on to make wise rulings, build God's temple, build his palace, and meet the Queen of Sheba. He was obedient to the Lord in most of his activities. However, he had a weakness for women and was not obedient about intermarrying with people who did not worship God. He had seven hundred wives and three hundred concubines. These women led him astray from worshiping God because he allowed their gods into his life. Solomon ruled forty years and his son Rehoboam succeeded him.

In the years following Solomon's reign came a slew of different kings who did not follow God. The temple was destroyed, then restored. All these kings had some sort of positive or negative spiritual effect on God's people.

May I be the leader at church, home, work, with my friends and with strangers that puts a smile on Your face. May I be the leader that sets the example daily by tearing down the idols of gossip, greed, slander, manipulation, jealously, fits of rage, selfish ambition, impurity, deception, vanity, negativity, laziness, procrastination, vengeance, pride, and the like. May I be the leader that uses wisdom only for Your glory. May I be the leader who remembers that what I say, what I do, and what I don't do affects or influences others. May I be the leader who never forgets where I was, where you have taken me, and the ultimate destination where you are pushing me. May I remember that even without an official title, I am a leader because we all are leaders in Your eyes!

May I be like David when he says in, I Chronicles 16:7-12:

Give praise to the Lord, proclaim his name; make known among the nations what he has done. Sing to him, sing praise to him; tell of all his wonderful acts. Glory in his holy name; let the hearts of those who seek the Lord rejoice. Look to the LORD and his strength; seek his face always. Remember the wonders he has done, his miracles, and the judgments he pronounced. . .

The Rocky Road

Before walking down the trail of poetry books and leaving God's historical books, I watched the builders of the Jerusalem wall. I watched them do God's will. In Nehemiah 3-7, each did their part in rebuilding the wall. Though many had skills unrelated with wall-building, they all helped rebuild the wall next to where they lived. Despite opposition and the need to bear arms, they built.

Nehemiah tells us how:

> . . .half of my men did the work, while the other half were equipped with spears, shields, bows and armor. The officers posted themselves behind all the people of Judah who were building the wall. Those who carried materials did their work with one hand and held a weapon in the other, and each of the builders wore his sword at his side as he worked. (Nehemiah 4:16-18)

Day and night, they worked on this wall – ordinary men. This ruined wall around an entire city was rebuilt because God put it on Nehemiah's heart to pray about it and take on the task of rebuilding the wall around His people. With God, everything is possible. "So, the wall was completed on the twenty-fifth of the Elul, in fifty-two days." (Nehemiah 6:15). *Fifty-two* days in a time of less technology than we have today around an entire city! *Fifty-two* days by ordinary men! *Fifty-two* days of building and fighting opposition against others who did not want this wall built! *Fifty-two* days of hard work and lack of sleep. *Fifty-two* days of danger! *Fifty-two* days of prayer! *Fifty-two* days of unity!

Being a part of God's Kingdom is just like building this wall. He uses each one of us through the talents He gives us to do His will. All we need to do is answer His call and do the work together as one unit – with one purpose. The way will be hard. Sometimes we will wonder, why did we take on this task and will want to quit. We will lose sleep. Daily we will arm ourselves with His Word against those who oppose us. Yet despite the improbability of the endeavor to which God calls us, the work can be done. Job reminds us in Job 42:2, as he spoke to God, "I know that you can do all things; no purpose of yours can be thwarted." Let us be builders of God's wall.

No matter what our gender, God uses us for His will. He used one of His women, Queen Esther. Through her tutelage from Mordecai and deep relationship with God, she allowed her faith in God to strengthen the people as she used her position against an edict issued by the king to destroy the Jews.

> Go, gather together all the Jews who are in Susa, and fast for me. Do not eat or drink for three days, night or day. I and my attendants will fast as you do. When this is done, I will go to the king, even though it is against the law. And if I perish, I perish. (Esther 4:16).

Approaching the king without his permission is punishable by death. Yet, God enabled her to petition the king, reveal Haman's plan, give honor to Mordecai, and save her people from annihilation.

Oh, my goodness, watching Job's complete commitment to God despite extreme loss is always mind-boggling. I cannot imagine having his kind of faith and commitment. I thought Abraham had faith, but this man, to me, went beyond Abraham in many ways. God allowed Satan to destroy everything Job had. He killed off all his children, burned up all his sheep and servants, had Chaldeans' raiding parties steal his sheep, had all his oxen and donkeys taken by the Sabeans, and killed the servants tending these animals. When Job heard all this, instead of moaning, groaning, and asking God why, he tore his clothes, shaved, and said:

> Naked I came from my mother's womb, and naked I will depart. The LORD gave and the LORD has taken away; may the name of the LORD be praised. Job 1:21.

What? Are you kidding me? That is only a response a faithful man of God would say. Then on top of all that God allowed Satan to touch the man up close and personal. Satan inflicted him with painful sores from the top of his head to the soles of his feet. Job used broken pieces of pottery to scrape himself while he sat in ashes. That sounds so miserable. Yet he sinned not.

His wife and friends were no help. "His wife said to him, "Are you still maintaining your integrity? Curse God and die!" (Job 2:9). His friends made it seem like he must have done some great sin to anger God. This turned into a heated discourse with his friends. There was no comfort anywhere for Job.

Job, however, was a~~ human like us. He did not like his situation. He bemoaned his birth that enabled all this to happen, even though God was the One who created him and gave him everything he had. Because Job did not sin, God gave him twice as much as he had before, and Job lived to see the fourth generation. Anytime I suffer physically about something, I must keep Job in mind and not sin against God. Anything He allows to happen to me, or my family physically is in His will and for His purpose. He will enable me to endure through it.

The majority of the first forty psalms are attributed to David and other writers praising God despite the dramas that happened in their lives. These psalms remind us how we must respond when the world encroaches upon us and brings misery to our lives. Intentionally being joyful is a choice we can make when we walk hand in hand with our Lord.

WEEK SEVEN – PSALMS 41 TO PROVERBS 31

The Road to Peace

Part of this week's Bible journey occurred while driving across country through the book of Psalms. I traveled with a family moving from Ohio to California. On day two of the six-day trek one of the vehicles simply stopped on the highway. We had to stay overnight in a small town while the car was being repaired.

At times I thought "The wicked have set a snare for me" (Psalm 119:110a). We received less than quality service at a restaurant. At our motel, we were told we could not have an extension of time to wait on our car, though there was no one else in the inn. We were homeless with only a moving truck for transportation. The eight of us with a cat and turtle had to walk everywhere. Our departure time loomed unknown before us as we waited.

What amazed me about this whole experience was how God's presence was there. Though we were not happy with our situation, you could tell that this was happening:

> The Lord watches over you—the Lord is your shade at your right hand; the sun will not harm you by day, nor the moon by night. Psalm 121:5-6.

There was a sense of peace and calmness while we waited. The children were not antsy. There was no sense of impatience or anger on the part of any of the adults. We all knew this was God's itinerary. We had to wait for Him to say when it was time to go. There was so much calmness that one of the workers commented on how well behaved the children and the pets were. I bet she probably wanted to say how calm the adults were as well. I can imagine the fits of rage she has seen while others have waited. She was so taken aback by us that she watched the pets while we went to dinner.

This stop took almost twenty-four hours out of our planned itinerary. Despite the time loss, we got to California at the scheduled arrival time. I believe it was because we all had this similar thought in mind: "My heart is set on keeping your decrees to the very end." (Psalm 119:112). No matter what happens – Jesus is Lord!

I love Proverbs. Proverbs is a book that convicts and holds nothing back. I belong to a mature women's group. Anytime someone begins to talk about Proverbs, we all say in a deep voice, *"Proverbs!"* because we know we are about to get a spanking.

No one can escape the clear "you better get it right" messages in Proverbs.

> The proverbs of Solomon son of David, king of Israel:
>
> for gaining wisdom and instruction;
>   for understanding words of insight;
> for receiving instruction in prudent behavior,
>   doing what is right and just and fair;
> for giving prudence to those who are simple,
>   knowledge and discretion to the young—
> let the wise listen and add to their learning,
>   and let the discerning get guidance—
> for understanding proverbs and parables,
>   the sayings and riddles of the wise.
>
> (Proverbs 1:1-7)

Proverbs dives into the benefits of answering wisdom's call at any cost. It warns against adultery and foolishness. In Chapters 10 to 29, Solomon writes a list of sages to direct the reader into acceptable behavior patterns. This part always stings and is the reason we say "*Proverbs!*" in a deep voice. Included in chapter 22:17-24, and chapter 34 are sayings of the wise. Chapter 30 contains the sayings of Agur son of Jakeh. Chapter 31 contains the sayings by King Lemuel that his mother taught him.

Chapter 31:10-31 is the epilogue of the book about the wife of noble character. As one who fulfills the roles of a wife, mother, businesswoman, church board member, and others, I am encouraged by this chapter on how to serve where God places me.

> Many women do noble things, but you surpass them all. Charm is deceptive, and beauty is fleeting; but a woman who fears the LORD is to be praised. Honor her for all that her hands have done, and let her works bring her praise at the city gate. (Proverbs 31:29-31).

May the books of Psalms and Proverbs be our guide for peaceful behavior as we walk in this world of strife.

What Time Is It?

Sitting here alone among the nature of the backyard given to me, I had a chance to reflect on this week's trek through Ecclesiastes, Song of Songs, and half of Isaiah.

The Fourth of July weekend was spent with visiting family from California and with local family. The time with family near and far was a cherished time for me.

- There is a time for everything and a season for every activity under the heavens. (Ecclesiastes 3:1).
- It was "a time to laugh". (Ecclesiastes 3:4).
- It was "a time to build" relationships. (Ecclesiastes. 3:3).
- It was "a time to dance". (Ecclesiastes 3:4).
- It was "a time to mourn" missing loved ones. (Ecclesiastes 3:4).
- It was "a time to embrace and a time to refrain." (Ecclesiastes 3:5).
- It was "a time to be silent and a time to speak." (Ecclesiastes 3:7).
- It was "a time to love. . . and a time for peace". (Ecclesiastes 3:8).

With the addition of two cousins who flew in from California, many members of our family were able to gather for several days. Because of these two cousins, my Bible trek moved at a slower pace than in the prior weeks. Because of the knowledge, enthusiasm, and youth of these two cousins, I have been greatly enriched. Because of these two cousins, God reinforced a message presented to me a few weeks ago – that it was time for another change.

For over ten years, I have worn my hair in braids. For more than five years, I wore the braids with extensions in them. The past five years, I wore braids with black beads at the end of the braids without extensions. The purpose of the braids has been for convenience. Though I have loved wearing them, they have been a source of confinement at the same time. I have always loved changing my hair look at a moment's notice.

There was a time when I found my braids to be the best fashion response to a period of weeks when I was literally in the deep waters of a pool or ocean with a scuba regulator or snorkel in my mouth. That volume of time in the water no longer exists. As with all things in life, there is a beginning and there is an end. Through the gentle words of a coworker, I was given the message the end of the beads was near.

Through the encouragement of the cousins, I finally acted upon a desire to know what the actual length of my hair is when completely straight. I knew a few weeks prior that the beads were leaving; but I thought I would keep the braids without beads. Once the experiment of seeing and feeling my hair straight was complete, I knew the braids were not coming back. The time for beads and braids was gone. It was time for straight hair. Wow, me in straight hair?! This is different. It is a challenge! It is no longer convenient. But whenever God says it is time – it is time! "Trust in the Lord forever, for the Lord, the Lord is the Rock eternal." (Isaiah 26:4).

Solomon talks about the meaningless of things we do in life and that there is nothing new under the sun. Solomon's Song of Songs are wedding songs of two lovers and their friends' involvement. Isaiah warns about events to come and gave godly counsel to many kings and people whether they wanted to hear it or not.

Even though Song of Songs is, on the surface, about two lovers, it helps us to see how our marriage with God should be. Do I always think deeply and endearingly about God? Do I long for His presence wherever I am? Do I miss Him when it seems the troubles in life make Him seem far away, when it is really me who is far from Him? How hard do I search for Him or do I accept living without Him?

> All night long on my bed I looked for the one my heart loves; I looked for him but did not find him. I will get up now and go about the city, through its streets and squares; I will search for the one my heart loves. So I looked for him but did not find him. The watchmen found me as they made their rounds in the city. "Have you seen the one my heart loves?" Scarcely had I passed them when I found the one my heart loves. I held him and would not let him go till I had brought him to my mother's house, to the room of the one who conceived me. (Song of Songs 3:1-4).

May we always keep Him the focus of our lives and not the distractions of this world.

Distractions Along the Way

Distractions! Distractions! Distractions! For the past two weeks, while slowly walking through the books of the prophets, I have been distracted! I have been distracted by things I created and things that were created by others. The days have been full, and the hours of sleep have been less. Time with family, time spent with hubby, extra hours spent on both jobs, maintenance of a new hairdo in the summer heat, dragon boat practices and learning the features of a new cell phone have been a few of the distractions. Those distractions have put me a week behind in my trek through the bible.

Reading the books of Isaiah and Jeremiah I often wondered, what type of prophecy can be said about me and my walk with God? Would it have the same warnings and reminders given in these two books?

> Now then, listen, you lover of pleasure, lounging in your security and saying to yourself, "I am, and there is none besides me. I will never be a widow or suffer the loss of children." Both of these will overtake you in a moment, on a single day: loss of children and widowhood. They will come upon you in full measure, in spite of your many sorceries and all your potent spells. You have trusted in your wickedness and have said, "No one sees me." Your wisdom and knowledge mislead you when you say to yourself, "I am, and there is none besides me." Disaster will come upon you, and you will not know how to conjure it away. A calamity will fall upon you that you cannot ward off with a ransom; a catastrophe you cannot foresee will suddenly come upon you. (Isaiah 47:8-11)

Am I letting the distractions of life make me "lax in doing the Lord's work!"? (Jeremiah 48:10). Are those distractions keeping me from having daily quality quiet times with Him? Are those distractions preventing me from listening to Him through His Word? Are those distractions silencing my lips from speaking to Him in prayer? Are those distractions squelching my desire to testify about Him to many? Are those distractions interfering with the plans God has for me?

> He has envisioned much for me.
> "For I know the plans I have for you," declares the Lord, "plans to prosper you and not to harm you, plans to give you hope and a future. Then you will call on me and come and pray to me, and I will listen to you. You will seek me and find me when you seek me with all your heart. I will be found by you." (Jeremiah 29:11-14).

This is one of my favorite scriptures. This encourages me when life's dramas overwhelm me, and my eyes want to stare at my problems instead of into the eyes of my Savior Jesus. His plans are always more than I can imagine, and His timing is perfect. May the distractions of life not distract me from God and the plans He created for me.

Messengers Trekking Along

This week's journey was full! My foot trekked through fifteen chapters: Lamentations, Ezekiel, Daniel, Hosea, Joel, Amos, Obadiah, Jonah, Micah, Nahum, Habakkuk, Zephaniah, Haggai, Zechariah, and Malachi. This also concluded the Old Testament part of this journey. Twelve of these chapters are the minor prophets (the last twelve). All of them are short and tell of how they were used to relay God's message to kings and people. They were all human and all of them had personal struggles with their walk with God.

Daniel, Hananiah, Mishael, and Azariah were ordered into service for the king to learn the language and literature of the Babylonians. They were to be trained for three years and then serve the king. Their names were changed: Daniel to Belteshazzar; Hananiah to Shadrach; Mishael to Meshach and Azariah to Abednego. These four men lives were changed forever, and they could do nothing about it.

They were told to eat the king's diet, which included foods that would defile them against God. With God's help, Daniel was able to convince the guard over them to allow them to eat vegetables and water for ten days. After the ten days, it was clear that they were healthier and more nourished than those who had eaten the king's diet. So, they were allowed to continue with a diet of vegetables and water. At the end of the three years, no one was more knowledgeable and wiser than they were. (Daniel 1).

So much more happened with these four men:

- Daniel was the only one able to interpret two of Nebuchadnezzar's dreams.
- Shadrach, Meshack and Abednego survived a blazing furnace after they refused to bow down to the golden image created by the king. Nothing was to be said against their God after this by anyone.
- Daniel was able to interpret a writing on a wall from God.
- Daniel survived an overnight stay in a den of lions after he continued to worship God, which was in violation of an edict from the king.

My deepest hurts in life descend upon me from my closest and most trusted friends and family members! Zipping through the remaining bible prophets brought to the surface of my brain memories of those times. They are times that I would prefer to forget or wish had never happened!

Micah drove this point home by telling me:

> Do not trust a neighbor; put no confidence in a friend. Even with the woman who lies in your embrace be careful of your words. For a son dishonors his father, a daughter rises up against her mother, a daughter-in-law against her mother-in-law—your enemies are the members of your own household. But as for me, I watch in hope for the Lord. I wait for God my Savior, my God will hear me. (Micah 7:5-7).

Wow! When I put my trust in man instead of God, it never turns out good. Putting my trust in something that is imperfect like I am sets me up for many a tearful night.

God tells me how to react when He calls – do what He says. Hosea tells me what God said to him when He called.

> The Lord said to me, "Go show your love to your wife again, though she is loved by another and is an adulteress. Love her as the Lord loves the Israelites, though they turn to other gods and love the sacred raisin cakes." Hosea 3:1.

Anytime God calls me to a mission, it is never easy! His call always demands a reliance on Him.

Jonah ran from God when He called. God wanted him to "Go to the great city of Nineveh and preach against it, because its wickedness has come up before me." (Jonah 1:2). Jonah did not want any parts of that and fled. He jumped on a ship going in another direction. A storm came up and the crew threw him overboard because Jonah eventually revealed to them he was the reason for the storm.

The storm ceased once he was thrown out. Then Jonah was swallowed by a huge fish and stayed there for three days. During those three days Jonah prayed to God and repented and said he would do God's will and he did.

I have done the same thing. I ignored God's command to stop being a travel agency owner. I loved being a travel agent and could not understand why. Instead, I kept doing what I wanted for two years. During that two years I had the largest group booking ever. The commission was going to be huge! Shortly before the final payment by the customers were due, I noticed I forgot to include a cost in their booking. There was no way I was going to ask the customer for that money this late in their plans. I had to eat it; which meant I owed the tour operator for this expenditure. In that moment of grief, I threw my hands up and said, "I give God! I will do what You want!" I felt a huge weight lift off my shoulders that I did not realize I was carrying. God's math is different than my math. Somehow, I received a tiny commission instead of owing. Now anytime God calls, I answer immediately. Delayed obedience is disobedience.

God loves me despite how I hurt Him repeatedly. He does not discard me or give up on me. He wants me to love others the way He loves me, even if those others do not love me! He also wants me to behave so that "As you have done, it will be done to you; your deeds will return upon your own head." (Obadiah 15b). He wants me to love, respect and treat others as I want to be loved, respected, and treated.

What a tall order God demands of us as His messengers. "He has shown all you people what is good. And what does the Lord require of you? To act justly and to love mercy and to walk humbly with your God." (Micah 6:8).

I Am with You

A desire of my heart was granted, but not in a way I had dreamed it would be!

One of my employers sent me to Portland, OR for continuing professional education. I was thrilled because this was one of the states needed in my fifty-state quest. I was ecstatic that my husband, Dan, could come because I'd accumulated enough frequent flyer miles...or so I thought. Much to my disappointment, I learned that the airline had changed their frequent flyer miles rules and Dan was not able to come. Since I had already made plans to stay an extra day because of Dan's anticipated stay, I decided to stay the extra day alone and go on a tour package of Mt. Hood. Vacationing without my spouse was something I had never done. I kept thinking, *what if I do not ever get to that state again? How can I be there and not "see" what God has created out there?* I hate living with regrets; I did not want this to be another one, something I should have done but did not.

During the week I contacted the top three tour operators. Two of them could not accommodate me because they did not have the minimum number of people needed for a tour. The third was out of business. I could not believe this. I had an extra day to tour and nowhere to go. Thoughts of renting a car and doing a self-drive tour came to mind. However, at the same time before and during this trip, a nagging nudge kept prodding me; "Do you really need to be doing this?" *I know! I know, my husband has been laid off for sixteen months.* Is this a wise use of God's money? *But I wanna see the waterfalls, the mountains, and the gorge.* By the time I got the third "no" from a tour operator, I finally got God's message: "Change your flight and get back home on Friday instead of Saturday". The extra cost of hotel, tours, food, and rental car was not acceptable! Of course, I could have been stiff-necked and rented that car and did it myself. But I do not think it would have gone well. I found out from another coworker that she was able to get one of the tours I was not able to because she waited for the slots to be filled. If I had waited, I would have gotten that tour with her. But would this use of money please God?

Though I did not get to see more of Oregon, God laid me out on my first day. He gave me the clearest day ever so that I could see Mt. Hood while making our descent into Portland. It is not normally clear in Portland at 10:30 a.m. I saw the mountain as we approached, as we flew on top of it and as we flew away from it with such detail and clarity, better than any tour would have given me!

I am joyful that His Word keeps me focused on (Luke 9:23-26):

> Whoever wants to be my disciple must deny themselves and take up their cross daily and follow me. For whoever wants to save their life will lose it, but whoever loses their life for me will save it. What good is it for you to gain the whole world *(tour experience),* and yet lose or forfeit your very self?

I can only serve one God; and that is by using the money He gives me wisely. "Either you will hate the one and love the other, or you will be devoted to the one and despise the other. You cannot serve both God and Money." (Luke 16:13).

This week's trek was all about Jesus in Matthew, Mark, Luke, and the first six chapters of John, the books of the Gospels. Each book told me about His life, His family, His disciples, His temptations, how He healed people, the miracles He did, the miracles He did not do, how He was betrayed, how He was abused, how He suffered a bloody death on a cross, how He rose from the dead. His purpose for leaving heaven and being born into a human form was to save us from our sins and to live with Him eternally. This is where my focus should always be -- doing that which glorifies Him and help others make the decision to dwell with Him.

> Then Jesus came to them and said, "All authority in heaven and on earth has been given to me. Therefore go and make disciples of all nations, baptizing them in the name of the Father and of the Son and of the Holy Spirit, and teaching them to obey everything I have commanded you. And surely I am with you always, to the very end of the age." (Matthew 28:18-20).

The Public Figure

While lingering in the books of the Gospels, the early church, and stepping into the first book of the Letters, I am heedful to what my thoughts and actions are.

What is my public life like as a coworker, parent, friend, spouse, family member, or associate? "No one who wants to become a public figure acts in secret. Since you are doing these things, show yourself to the world." (John 7:4). Even though I am not a politician or actress, I live among people, so I am a public figure!

- As a public figure, what do I believe about God?

  In the beginning was the Word, and the Word was with God, and the Word was God. He was with God in the beginning. Through him all things were made; without him nothing was made that has been made. In him was life, and that life was the light of all mankind. The light shines in the darkness, and the darkness has not overcome it. (John 1:1-5).

- As a public figure, am I pointing fingers?

Let any one of you who is without sin be the first to throw a stone at her. (John 8:7).

- As a public figure, do I trust in God or self?

  Do not let your hearts be troubled. Trust in God. (John 14:1).

- As a public figure, am I sharing with those in need?

  All the believers were one in heart and mind. No one claimed that any of their possessions was their own, but they shared everything they had. . .there was no needy person among them. (Acts 4: 32 and 34).

- As a public figure, what do I believe?

  This is why "It was credited to him as righteousness." The words "it was credited to him" were written not for him alone, but also for us to whom God will credit righteousness—for us who believe in him who raised Jesus our Lord from the dead. (Romans 4:22-24).

- As a public figure, am I a slave to the ways of man or the ways of God?

But now by dying to what once bound us, we have been released from the law so that we serve in the new way of the Spirit, and not in the old way of the written code. (Romans 7:6).

- As a public figure, am I open to continual change and refreshment?

  Do not conform to the pattern of this world, but be transformed by the renewing of your mind. Then you will be able to test and approve what God's will is—his good, pleasing and perfect will. (Romans 12:2)

- As a public figure, am I submissive to authority?

  The authorities that exist have been established by God. Consequently, whoever rebels against the authority is rebelling against what God has instituted, and those who do so will bring judgment on themselves. (Romans 13:1-2).

- As a public figure, am I judgmental?

> You then, why do you judge your brother or sister? Or why do you treat your brother or sister with contempt? For we all will stand before God's judgment seat. . .we will all give an account of ourselves to God. (Romans 14:10 and 12).

May we remember that we are public figures everywhere we are, even in our thoughts.

Scattered Letters

Taking you with me on this adventure was challenging yet invigorating. The last part of this journey is akin to Week Ten when fifteen chapters were read. This week, twenty-one chapters were read: 1 and 2 Corinthians; Galatians; Ephesians; Philippians; Colossians; 1 and 2 Thessalonians; 1 and 2 Timothy; Titus; Philemon; Hebrews; James; 1 and 2 Peter; 1, 2 and 3 John; Jude; and Revelations.

Fourteen of the twenty-one Letters in the Bible are associated with Paul's writings. However, seven of them are undisputed as to Paul being the author: Romans, 1 and 2 Corinthians, Galatians, Philippians, 1 Thessalonians and Philemon. The other letters strongly point to Paul as the author but are not authenticated: Ephesians, Colossians, 2 Thessalonians, 1 and 2 Timothy, Titus, and Hebrews. His letters were written to churches and individuals to educate, strengthen, encourage, or discipline.

Paul reminds me in his letter to not allow divisions in the church as he spoke to the Corinthian church:

I appeal to you, brothers and sisters, in the name of our Lord Jesus Christ, that all of you agree with one another in what you say and that there be no divisions among you, but that you be perfectly united in mind and thought. My brothers and sisters, some from Chloe's household have informed me that there are quarrels among you. What I mean is this: One of you says, "I follow Paul"; another, "I follow Apollos"; another, "I follow Cephas"; still another, "I follow Christ."

Is Christ divided? Was Paul crucified for you? Were you baptized in the name of Paul? I thank God that I did not baptize any of you except Crispus and Gaius, so no one can say that you were baptized in my name. (Yes, I also baptized the household of Stephanas; beyond that, I don't remember if I baptized anyone else.) For Christ did not send me to baptize, but to preach the gospel—not with wisdom and eloquence, lest the cross of Christ be emptied of its power. (I Corinthians 1:10-17).

Paul did not pull any punches when he pointed out blatant sin.

> It is actually reported that there is sexual immorality among you, and of a kind that even pagans do not tolerate: A man is sleeping with his father's wife. And you are proud! Shouldn't you rather have gone into mourning and have put out of your fellowship the man who has been doing this? (I Corinthians 5:1-2).

He warns about sin and not to fall prey to it.

> So I say, walk by the Spirit, and you will not gratify the desires of the flesh. For the flesh desires what is contrary to the Spirit, and the Spirit what is contrary to the flesh. They are in conflict with each other, so that you are not to do whatever you want. But if you are led by the Spirit, you are not under the law.
>
> The acts of the flesh are obvious: sexual immorality, impurity and debauchery; idolatry and witchcraft; hatred, discord, jealousy, fits of rage, selfish ambition, dissensions, factions and envy; drunkenness, orgies, and the like. I warn you, as I did before, that those who live like this will not inherit the kingdom of God.

(Galatians 5:16-21).

When I am dealing with struggles in my relationships, health, or anything else unpleasant, this is my favorite go-to scripture.

> Consider it pure joy, my brothers and sisters, whenever you face trials of many kinds, because you know that the testing of your faith produces perseverance. Let perseverance finish its work so that you may be mature and complete, not lacking anything. If any of you lacks wisdom, you should ask God, who gives generously to all without finding fault, and it will be given to you. But when you ask, you must believe and not doubt, because the one who doubts is like a wave of the sea, blown and tossed by the wind. That person should not expect to receive anything from the Lord. Such a person is double-minded and unstable in all they do. (James 1:2-8).

As I continue to learn the person that I am, in whatever hairdo and less weight I wear, I must keep in mind:

> Your beauty should not come from outward adornment, such as elaborate hairstyles and the wearing of gold jewelry and fine clothes. Rather, it should be that of your inner self, the unfading beauty of a gentle and quiet spirit, which is of great worth in God's sight." (I Peter 3:3-4).

It was encouraging to remember that by adding to my faith, goodness, knowledge, self-control, perseverance, godliness, mutual affection, and love, that I will keep "from being ineffective and unproductive in your knowledge of our Lord Jesus Christ." and "will never stumble" and "will receive a rich welcome into the eternal kingdom of our Lord." (2 Peter 1:5-8, 10-11).

Pride is the root of many of my issues. According to scriptures,

> God opposes the proud but shows favor to the humble and oppressed. Submit yourselves, then, to God. Resist the devil, and he will flee from you. Come near to God and he will come near to you. . .Humble yourselves before the Lord, and he will lift you up. (James 4:6-8, 10).

Paul talked about so many things in his letters: married life relationships, sexual immorality, lawsuits among believers, virgins, warnings, orderly worship, spiritual gifts, love, speaking in tongues, Christ, resurrection when Jesus returns, tithing, his travels, persecution, imprisonment, forgiveness, faith, and so much more. No matter what Paul endured, he stayed focused on his mission to preach the Gospel to everyone he met. May we, too, keep our eyes fixed on Jesus in all parts of our lives and use His Word as our guidebook.

Juel A Fitzgerald has been writing since she was a youngster. Her earliest efforts included working at her high school newspaper, then with different college publications. She has a bachelor's degree in English from Kent State University in Kent, Ohio.

Because of God's prompting she started blogging in 2010 and now has four active blogs. The first blog is a weekly spiritual devotional. The second is a travel blog. The third is a walking blog about raising funds for HOPE *worldwide*. The fourth is a writer's blog.

Her first book was published in June 2020, "Lives of a Gem! God's Treasured Possession". This book is an inspirational and transparent memoir about how God walked her through spiritual and physical life challenges. Another book published in 2021, "The Twelve: Fishers of Men" gives you a glimpse of the lives of the first twelve disciples.

She is a thirty-seven-year government retiree. During that span, she worked with the Internal Revenue Service, the Veterans Administration Hospital, and the Navy Finance Department. She is also a seventeen-year travel agent retiree. In addition, she is a five-year retired Weight Watchers Leader.

Her love of public speaking materialized due to Toastmasters. She has had numerous teaching and speaking assignments with the Boy Scouts and Girl Scouts, with the government, in the travel industry and as a Weight Watchers Leader. She has been married forty-six years, has two adult children, and two grandchildren.

Her focus is to do **all for His glory, live His schedule,** and **pray Big!**

Juel's Creations, LLC.
P. O. Box 221172
Beachwood, OH 44122
https://juelscreations.com/

www.ingramcontent.com/pod-product-compliance
Lightning Source LLC
Chambersburg PA
CBHW060411080526
44583CB00012B/530